CANDIDA ON ICE

20+ sugar-free ice creams and cold treats

PAULA MILLER - WHOLE INTENTIONS

COPYRIGHT

As you create the recipes in this book, we encourage you to share it with friends and family. However, out of respect for the law, and the work that went into this book, we ask that you not give away the entire book, but instead encourage others to purchase their own copy at http://candidaonice.com.

This entire publication is protected under the U.S. Copyright Act of 1976 and all other applicable international, federal, state and local laws, and all rights are reserved, including resale rights. You are not allowed to give or sell this book to anyone else without paying for it.

Any trademarks, service marks, product names or named features are assumed to be the property of their respective owners, and are used only for reference. There is no implied endorsement if I use one of these terms. Copyright © 2017 Paula Miller. All rights reserved worldwide.

If you have questions about the appropriate use of recipes from this book on your website, please contact me at paula@wholeintentions.com.

© 2017 | All rights reserved.

Candida on Ice | candidaonice.com

Too Long Ignored. . .

I was sitting in my home office, staring at my computer screen, and looking at a word I'd ignored for seven years.

My eyes flew across the page, reading as fast as I could, and feeling both a sinking sensation and a flutter of hope in my chest.

Candida.

I called Travis over and showed him the information I was reading. We looked at each other solemnly. "I think candida might be more serious than we ever gave it credit for."

~~~~~

Hi, I'm Paula. Our candida journey, like most people's, started long before we even knew what candida was.

If fact, that journey starts from the time we're born. Whether or not you were born cesarean or vaginally, whether you suffered from repeated childhood illnesses and were given antibiotics, what your eating habits are like. . . decisions we don't even think about are the breeding ground for a possible candida invasion.

When we were first told by our naturopath that my husband Travis had candida and Lyme disease, we ignored the candida and focused solely on the Lyme. What we didn't realize though, was that ignoring it was only making it worse.

We tried to eat health-IER to help Travis's immunity, we avoided the foods he was allergic to, we visited a clinic that specialized in Lyme disease. . .but, while all that helped, it didn't help us understand that our gut played a much bigger role in our health than we realized.

By the time the word 'candida' came up again seven years later, we knew we needed to take the time to research it and take it seriously.

And as you've probably come to realize - taking it seriously means taking your diet seriously. Knowing that you have to drastically cut out sugar, even natural sugar like honey or maple syrup, might not be difficult for some, but for the rest of us, it's a hard pill to swallow!

Candida on Ice was made for those special occasions that call for a nice bowl of ice cream or a cold treat on a hot summer day - without feeding your candida.

If you have any questions about candida or these particular recipes, you can visit my site, Whole Intentions.com, or contact me at paula@wholeintentions.com.

Paula

Helpful Tips

Ice cream is delicious no matter the season - but when your season of life is dealing with candida, it's not fun giving it up! But now you don't have to!

Candida on Ice is made specifically for those dealing with candida and gut health issues and various allergies, those who want to avoid sugars and refined carbohydrates, those who want to eat healthier and lose weight...

These cold and frozen treats can be enjoyed by all - and without making your health worse. We've had so much fun making the recipes in this book - and we learned a lot! Here are some of our favorite tips:

1. There are many brands of stevia. You'll want to look for the ones that don't have a lot of 'added' ingredients like erythritol, maltodextrin, and dextrose. The best bet is to look for whole leaf stevia or brands that are 100% stevia without added fillers. Some of my favorite brands are Now Foods Better Stevia, Liquid and Now Foods Better Stevia, Powder.

2. Some stevia brands are sweeter than others, some have an aftertaste - and how sweet we like our treats depends on the individual. This makes it hard to specify measurements in a recipe. I've used the measurements that my family likes, but each recipe says 'to taste' for a reason.

   My suggestion would be to first cut the amount of stevia in the recipe in half - then add just a little at a time and taste test. You'll want the recipe to be just a tad sweeter than you like it because freezing (or baking for that matter) will dull the sweetness. Remember, these recipes were made to my family's taste - but you might want them just a tad sweeter or maybe less vanilla-y. Feel free to change them up to suit your tastes.

3. Stevia and salt are bosom buddies. Nearly every recipe calls for 'a pinch of celtic sea salt' and 'stevia to taste'. We do that because they compliment each other nicely. :)

4. Xylitol doesn't dissolve as easily as refined white sugar, so we measure it out first, then grind it in a small electric coffee grinder or high-powered blender so it's more like powdered sugar. Even if a recipe's directions tell you to mix everything in a blender, the granules won't dissolve as well as they do when powdered, so we still recommend grinding it first.

5. You'll see that we use two kinds of milk for most of our recipes. We use canned unsweetened coconut milk (we like Thai brand) which is thick with lots of cream

and works like a heavy whipping cream. We also use unsweetened nut milk alternatives such as coconut, almond, and cashew.

6. We used a Cuisanart Ice Cream Maker to make our ice creams, but if you don't have one, you can easily pour the mixture into a small, deep pan, like a bread pan, and freeze for 2-3 hours.

7. All of our ice creams can be eaten right out of the ice cream maker, as soon as they've thickened. You can also pour the finished ice cream into a freezer safe bowl and freeze for 2-3 hours for a more solid ice cream. If you do this, you'll want to let it sit out for about 20 min. until it's scoop-able.

Recipe Index

ICE CREAM 1

    Vanilla 2

    Chocolate 3

    Strawberry 4

    Chocolate Chunk Cookie Dough 7

    Butter Pecan 11

    Berry Blast 13

    Joyous Almond Delight 15

    Mint Chocolate Chunk 18

    Maple Nut 21

    Snickerdoodle 23

    Cinna-Coffee Bun 24

    Cookies N' Cream Madness 27

ICE TREATS 31

    Avocado Pudding Pops 32

    Instant Strawberry Slush 33

    Healthy Lemonade Popsicles 34

    Pau D' Arco Popsicles 35

    Eggnog Dessert 37

    Butterscotch-Vanilla Float 39

    Candida-Dilly Bars 40

ICE CREAM

Vanilla

- 1 - 14 oz. unsweetened canned coconut milk
- 1 c. unsweetened nut milk (coconut, almond, cashew, etc.)
- 4 T. vanilla extract
- 1/4 c. xylitol granules, powdered
- a pinch of celtic sea salt
- 1/2 tsp. stevia, or to taste

Directions:

8. Measure xylitol first, and then grind it in a small electric coffee grinder or high powered blender (the coffee grinder makes a finer powder). Then combine canned coconut milk, nut milk, vanilla extract, xylitol powder, and salt and blend thoroughly.

9. Add the stevia to the mixture - start with half of the stevia the recipe calls for, then add a little at a time until it's almost too sweet. (When the ice cream freezes, the sweetness factor subsides.)

10. Pour mixture into the bowl of an ice cream machine. Freeze according to the manufacturer's instructions. After the ice cream is thickened, you can eat it immediately or transfer it to an airtight container, cover tightly with a lid, and freeze until ready to serve.

    Optionally, you can also pour the ice cream mixture directly into a freezer-safe bowl, cover with a lid, and freeze without the need for an ice cream machine (however, the ice cream will not be as creamy).

11. Let ice cream sit at room temperature for about 20 minutes before serving.

Chocolate

- 1 - 14 oz. unsweetened canned coconut milk
- 1 c. unsweetened nut milk (coconut, almond, cashew, etc.)
- 1/2 c. raw cacao powder
- 1 T. vanilla extract
- 5 T. xylitol granules, powdered
- a pinch of celtic sea salt
- 1 tsp. stevia, or to taste

Directions:

1. Measure xylitol first, and then grind it in a small electric coffee grinder or high powered blender (the coffee grinder makes a finer powder). Then combine canned coconut milk, nut milk, cacao powder, vanilla extract, xylitol powder, and salt and blend thoroughly.

2. Add the stevia to the mixture - start with half of the stevia the recipe calls for, then add a little at a time until it's almost too sweet. (When the ice cream freezes, the sweetness factor subsides.)

3. Pour mixture into the bowl of an ice cream machine. Freeze according to the manufacturer's instructions. After the ice cream is thickened, you can eat it immediately or transfer it to an airtight container, cover tightly with a lid, and freeze until ready to serve.

   Optionally, you can also pour the ice cream mixture directly into a freezer-safe bowl, cover with a lid, and freeze without the need for an ice cream machine (however, the ice cream will not be as creamy).

4. Let ice cream sit at room temperature for about 20 minutes before serving.

Strawberry

- 1 - 14 oz. unsweetened canned coconut milk
- 1 c. unsweetened nut milk (coconut, almond, cashew, etc.)
- 2 c. frozen strawberries
- 2 T. vanilla extract
- 1/4 c. xylitol granules, powdered
- a pinch of celtic sea salt
- 1/2 tsp. stevia, or to taste

Directions:

1. Measure xylitol first, and then grind it in a small electric coffee grinder or high powered blender (the coffee grinder makes a finer powder). Then combine canned coconut milk, nut milk, frozen strawberries, vanilla extract, xylitol powder, and salt and blend thoroughly.

2. Add the stevia to the mixture - start with half of the stevia the recipe calls for, then add a little at a time until it's almost too sweet. (When the ice cream freezes, the sweetness factor subsides.)

3. Pour mixture into the bowl of an ice cream machine. Freeze according to the manufacturer's instructions. After the ice cream is thickened, you can eat it immediately or transfer it to an airtight container, cover tightly with a lid, and freeze until ready to serve.

    Optionally, you can also pour the ice cream mixture directly into a freezer-safe bowl, cover with a lid, and freeze without the need for an ice cream machine (however, the ice cream will not be as creamy).

4. Let ice cream sit at room temperature for about 20 minutes before serving.

Chocolate Chunk Cookie Dough

Part 1: Chocolate Chunks:
(Recipe from The Sweeter Side of Candida)

- 1 c. cocoa butter
- 1 c. raw cacao powder
- 1 tsp. vanilla extract
- 1/8 tsp. almond extract
- 1 T. butter, optional if casein-free
- 3 Tbs. xylitol granules, powdered
- pinch of celtic sea salt
- stevia to taste

Directions:

1. Melt the cocoa butter over low heat in a small saucepan.
2. Measure xylitol first, and then grind it in a small electric coffee grinder or high powered blender (the coffee grinder makes a finer powder). Add the xylitol powder to the cocoa butter.
3. Add the cacao powder, vanilla extract, almond extract, and butter (optional) to the saucepan.
4. Blend together, and then add the stevia to the mixture - start with half of the stevia the recipe calls for, then add a little at a time until it's almost too sweet. (When the ice cream freezes, the sweetness factor subsides.)
5. Bring to a light, simmering boil and then remove from heat. Let it cool a bit and then pour into 9x9 glass pan and put in freezer for about 1 hour or until hardened.

6. Once it's frozen, pop the chocolate out of the pan and put into a plastic zippered bag. Break it into chunks. Use half of the chunks to add to the cookie dough and save the other half for another recipe (like the Mint Chocolate Chunk ice cream!).

COOKIE DOUGH:
(Recipe from The Sweeter Side of Candida)

- 2 c. almond flour
- 1/4 c. butter, softened or coconut oil
- 1/2 c. xylitol granules, powdered
- 1/2 tsp. celtic sea salt
- 1 tsp. baking powder
- 3 tsp. vanilla extract
- 1/4 tsp. almond extract
- stevia to taste

Directions:

1. Measure out the xylitol and then grind it in a small electric coffee grinder or a high-powered blender.
2. Combine all the ingredients except the stevia into a medium mixing bowl. Add the xylitol powder to the mixture.
3. Add the stevia. Start with half of the stevia the recipe calls for, then add a little more at a time until it's almost too sweet. (When the dough freezes, the sweetness factor subsides.)
4. Stir in the chocolate chunks by hand until well combined.
5. Form small thumbnail-sized balls of cookie dough. Place in small bowl and freeze. You can use all of the dough for dough balls, or make the rest of the dough into cookies.

TO MAKE COOKIES:

1. Preheat the oven to 350 degrees. Line a baking sheet with parchment paper.

2. Form the leftover dough into golfball sized balls with your hands and place about 3" apart on lined baking sheet. Flatten the cookies slightly with the bottom of the glass or your hand.

3. Bake approximately 15-17 minutes. Let sit 5-10 minutes on the baking sheet before moving to a wire rack. Cool completely.

ICE CREAM:

- 1 - 14 oz. unsweetened canned coconut milk
- 1 c. unsweetened nut milk (coconut, almond, cashew, etc.)
- 4 T. vanilla extract
- 1/4 c. xylitol granules, powdered
- a pinch of celtic sea salt
- 1/2 tsp. stevia, or to taste

DIRECTIONS:

1. Measure xylitol first, and then grind it in a small electric coffee grinder or high powered blender (the coffee grinder makes a finer powder). Then combine canned coconut milk, nut milk, vanilla extract, xylitol powder, and salt and blend thoroughly.

2. Add the stevia to the mixture - start with half of the stevia the recipe calls for, then add a little at a time until it's almost too sweet. (When the ice cream freezes, the sweetness factor subsides.)

3. Pour mixture into the bowl of an ice cream machine. Freeze according to the manufacturer's instructions. After the ice cream is thickened, gently stir in the frozen cookie dough balls by hand. You can eat it immediately or transfer it to an airtight container. Cover tightly with a lid and freeze until ready to serve.

4. Optionally, you can also pour the ice cream mixture directly into a freezer-safe bowl, cover with a lid, and freeze without the need for an ice cream machine (however, the ice cream will not be as creamy).

5. Let ice cream sit at room temperature for about 20 minutes before serving.

Butter Pecan

- 1 - 14 oz. unsweetened canned coconut milk
- 1 c. unsweetened nut milk (coconut, almond, cashew, etc.)
- 2 eggs
- 1 tsp. vanilla extract
- 1/2 tsp. butter extract or 1 Tbs. butter
- 3/4 c. chopped pecans, toasted
- 1/4 c. xylitol granules, powdered
- a pinch of celtic sea salt
- 1 tsp. stevia, or to taste

Directions:

1. Place pecans on cookie sheet and toast at 325 degrees for 15 minutes until just lightly browned. Set aside to cool.

2. Measure xylitol first, and then grind it in a small electric coffee grinder or high powered blender (the coffee grinder makes a finer powder). Then combine canned coconut milk, nut milk, eggs, vanilla extract, butter extract (or butter), xylitol powder, and salt and blend thoroughly.

3. Pour mixture into a medium-sized sauce pan. Heat over medium heat, stirring constantly for 10 minutes. DO NOT BOIL. Set aside until cooled.

4. Add stevia to the cooled mixture. Start with half of the stevia the recipe calls for, then add a little at a time until it's almost too sweet. (When the ice cream freezes, the sweetness factor subsides.) Stir toasted pecans into mixture.

5. Pour mixture into the bowl of an ice cream machine. Freeze according to the manufacturer's instructions. After the ice cream is thickened, you can eat it immediately or transfer it to an airtight container, cover tightly with a lid, and freeze until ready to serve.

    Optionally, you can also pour the ice cream mixture directly into a freezer-safe bowl, cover with a lid, and freeze without the need for an ice cream machine (however, the ice cream will not be as creamy).

6. Let ice cream sit at room temperature for about 20 minutes before serving.

Berry Blast

- 1 - 14 oz. unsweetened canned coconut milk
- 1 c. unsweetened nut milk (coconut, almond, cashew, etc.)
- 12 oz. frozen mixed berries (e.g. strawberries,
- blueberries, raspberries, blackberries, etc.), divided
- 1 T. vanilla extract
- 1/2 tsp. almond extract
- 2 T. xylitol granules, powdered
- a pinch of celtic sea salt
- 1/4 tsp. stevia, or to taste

Directions:

1. Measure xylitol first, and then grind it in a small electric coffee grinder or high powered blender (the coffee grinder makes a finer powder). Then combine canned coconut milk, nut milk, 8 oz. frozen mixed berries, vanilla extract, almond extract, xylitol powder, and salt and blend thoroughly.

2. Add the stevia to the mixture - start with half of the stevia the recipe calls for, then add a little at a time until it's almost too sweet. (When the ice cream freezes, the sweetness factor subsides.)

3. Pour mixture into the bowl of an ice cream machine. Freeze according to the manufacturer's instructions. After the ice cream is thickened, gently stir in the last 4 oz. of frozen mixed berries by hand.

4. You can eat it immediately or transfer it to an airtight container, cover tightly with a lid, and freeze until ready to serve.

Optionally, you can also pour the ice cream mixture directly into a freezer-safe bowl, cover with a lid, and freeze without the need for an ice cream machine (however, the ice cream will not be as creamy).

5. Let ice cream sit at room temperature for about 20 minutes before serving.

Joyous Almond Delight

- 1 - 14 oz. unsweetened canned coconut milk
- 1 c. unsweetened nut milk (coconut, almond, cashew, etc.)
- 1/2 c. raw cacao powder
- 1 T. vanilla extract
- 1/2 tsp. almond extract
- 5 T. xylitol granules, powdered
- a pinch of celtic sea salt
- 1 tsp. stevia, or to taste
- 1/3 c. unsweetened coconut flakes, toasted
- 1/3 c. chopped almonds, toasted

Directions:

1. Place almonds on cookie sheet and toast at 325 degrees for 10 minutes. Remove pan, add the unsweetened coconut flakes to the almonds and bake an additional 5 to 7 minutes or until coconut flakes are just lightly browned. Set aside to cool.

2. Measure xylitol first, and then grind it in a small electric coffee grinder or high powered blender (the coffee grinder makes a finer powder). Then combine canned coconut milk, nut milk, cacao powder, vanilla extract, almond extract, xylitol powder, and salt and blend thoroughly.

3. Add the stevia to the mixture - start with half of the stevia the recipe calls for, then add a little at a time until it's almost too sweet. (When the ice cream freezes, the sweetness factor subsides.)

4. Add toasted almonds and coconut flakes to the mixture.

5. Pour mixture into the bowl of an ice cream machine. Freeze according to the manufacturer's instructions. After the ice cream is thickened, you can eat it immediately or transfer it to an airtight container, cover tightly with a lid, and freeze until ready to serve.

   Optionally, you can also pour the ice cream mixture directly into a freezer-safe bowl, cover with a lid, and freeze without the need for an ice cream machine (however, the ice cream will not be as creamy).

6. Let ice cream sit at room temperature for about 20 minutes before serving.

Mint Chocolate Chunk

CHOCOLATE CHUNKS:
(Recipe from The Sweeter Side of Candida)

- 1 c. cocoa butter
- 1 c. raw cacao powder
- 1 tsp. vanilla extract
- 1/8 tsp. almond extract
- 1 T. butter, optional if casein-free
- 3 Tbs. xylitol granules, powdered
- pinch of celtic sea salt
- stevia to taste

DIRECTIONS:

1. Melt the cocoa butter over low heat in a small saucepan.

2. Measure xylitol first, and then grind it in a small electric coffee grinder or high powered blender (the coffee grinder makes a finer powder). Add the xylitol powder to the cocoa butter.

3. Add the cacao powder, vanilla extract, almond extract, and butter (optional) to the saucepan.

4. Blend together, and then add the stevia to the mixture - start with half of the stevia the recipe calls for, then add a little at a time until it's almost too sweet. (When the ice cream freezes, the sweetness factor subsides.)

5. Bring to a light, simmering boil and then remove from heat. Let it cool a bit and then pour into 9x9 glass pan and put in freezer for about 1 hour or until hardened.

6. Once it's frozen, pop the chocolate out of the pan and put into a plastic zippered bag. Break it into chunks. Use half of the chunks to add to the cookie dough and save the other half for another recipe (like the Chocolate Chunk Cookie Dough ice cream!).

ICE CREAM:

- 1 - 14 oz. unsweetened canned coconut milk
- 1 c. unsweetened nut milk (coconut, almond, cashew, etc.)
- 2 avocados, peeled and seed removed
- 2 tsp. peppermint extract
- 3 T. xylitol granules, powdered
- a pinch of celtic sea salt
- 1 tsp. stevia, or to taste
- 1/2 of Chocolate Chunk Recipe

DIRECTIONS:

1. Measure xylitol first, and then grind it in a small electric coffee grinder or high powered blender (the coffee grinder makes a finer powder). Then combine canned coconut milk, nut milk, avocados, peppermint extract, xylitol powder, and salt and blend thoroughly.

2. Add the stevia to the mixture - start with half of the stevia the recipe calls for, then add a little at a time until it's almost too sweet. (When the ice cream freezes, the sweetness factor subsides.)

3. Pour mixture into the bowl of an ice cream machine. Freeze according to the manufacturer's instructions. After the ice cream is thickened, gently stir in the Chocolate Chunks by hand. You can eat it immediately or transfer it to an airtight container, cover tightly with a lid, and freeze until ready to serve.

4. Optionally, you can also pour the ice cream mixture directly into a freezer-safe bowl, cover with a lid, and freeze without the need for an ice cream machine (however, the ice cream will not be as creamy).

5. Let ice cream sit at room temperature for about 20 minutes before serving.

Maple Nut

- 1 - 14 oz. unsweetened canned coconut milk
- 1 c. unsweetened nut milk (coconut, almond, cashew, etc.)
- 2 eggs
- 2-3 tsp. maple extract
- 1 c. chopped walnuts, toasted
- 1/4 c. xylitol granules, powdered
- 1/2 tsp. celtic sea salt
- 1 tsp. stevia, or to taste

Directions:

1. Place walnuts on cookie sheet and toast at 325 degrees for 15 minutes until just lightly browned. Set aside to cool.

2. Measure xylitol first, and then grind it in a small electric coffee grinder or high powered blender (the coffee grinder makes a finer powder). Then combine canned coconut milk, nut milk, eggs, maple extract, xylitol powder, and salt and blend thoroughly.

3. Pour mixture into a medium-sized sauce pan. Heat over medium heat, stirring constantly for 10 minutes. DO NOT BOIL. Set aside until cooled.

4. Add the stevia to the mixture - start with half of the stevia the recipe calls for, then add a little at a time until it's almost too sweet. (When the ice cream freezes, the sweetness factor subsides.)

5. Stir toasted walnuts into mixture.

6. Pour mixture into the bowl of an ice cream machine. Freeze according to the manufacturer's instructions. After the ice cream is thickened, you can eat it immediately or transfer it to an airtight container, cover tightly with a lid, and freeze until ready to serve.

7. Optionally, you can also pour the ice cream mixture directly into a freezer-safe bowl, cover with a lid, and freeze without the need for an ice cream machine (however, the ice cream will not be as creamy).

8. Let ice cream sit at room temperature for about 20 minutes before serving.

Snickerdoodle

- 1 - 14 oz. unsweetened canned coconut milk
- 1 c. unsweetened nut milk (coconut, almond, cashew, etc.)
- 2 T. vanilla extract
- 2 tsp. cinnamon
- 1 tsp. nutmeg
- 1/4 c. xylitol granules, powdered
- a pinch of celtic sea salt
- 1/2 tsp. stevia, or to taste

Directions:

1. Measure xylitol first, and then grind it in a small electric coffee grinder or high powered blender (the coffee grinder makes a finer powder). Then combine canned coconut milk, nut milk, vanilla extract, cinnamon, nutmeg, xylitol powder, and salt and blend thoroughly.

2. Add the stevia to the mixture - start with half of the stevia the recipe calls for, then add a little at a time until it's almost too sweet. (When the ice cream freezes, the sweetness factor subsides.)

3. Pour mixture into the bowl of an ice cream machine. Freeze according to the manufacturer's instructions. After the ice cream is thickened, you can eat it immediately or transfer it to an airtight container, cover tightly with a lid, and freeze until ready to serve.

4. Optionally, you can also pour the ice cream mixture directly into a freezer-safe bowl, cover with a lid, and freeze without the need for an ice cream machine (however, the ice cream will not be as creamy).

5. Let ice cream sit at room temperature for about 20 minutes before serving.

Cinna-Coffee Bun

- 1 - 14 oz. unsweetened canned coconut milk
- 1 c. unsweetened nut milk (coconut, almond, cashew, etc.)
- 3 egg yolks
- 2 Tbs. instant coffee granules
- 1/4 tsp. cinnamon
- 1/4 c. + 2 Tbs. xylitol granules, powdered
- a pinch of celtic sea salt
- 1/2 tsp. stevia, or to taste

Directions:

1. Measure xylitol first, and then grind it in a small electric coffee grinder or high powered blender (the coffee grinder makes a finer powder). Then combine canned coconut milk, nut milk, egg yolks, coffee granules, cinnamon, xylitol powder, and salt and blend thoroughly.

2. Pour mixture into a medium-sized sauce pan. Heat over medium heat, stirring constantly for 10 minutes. DO NOT BOIL. Set aside until cooled.

3. Add the stevia to the mixture - start with half of the stevia the recipe calls for, then add a little at a time until it's almost too sweet. (When the ice cream freezes, the sweetness factor subsides.)

4. Pour mixture through a fine mesh strainer.

5. Pour strained mixture into the bowl of an ice cream machine. Freeze according to the manufacturer's instructions. After the ice cream is thickened, you can eat it immediately or transfer it to an airtight container, cover tightly with a lid, and freeze until ready to serve.

6. Optionally, you can also pour the ice cream mixture directly into a freezer-safe bowl, cover with a lid, and freeze without the need for an ice cream machine (however, the ice cream will not be as creamy).

7. Let ice cream sit at room temperature for about 20 minutes before serving.

Cookies N' Cream Madness

Chocolate Cookies/Crust:

- 1 c. almond flour
- 3 T. raw cacao powder
- 2 T. arrowroot powder
- 1 T. coconut flour
- 1/4 tsp. baking soda
- 1/4 c. xylitol granules, powdered
- 1 egg
- 2 T. coconut butter (a.k.a. coconut manna, coconut cream)
- pinch of celtic sea salt

Directions for cookies:

1. Measure xylitol first, and then grind it in a small electric coffee grinder or high powered blender (the coffee grinder makes a finer powder).

2. With a fork, combine almond flour, cacao powder, arrowroot powder, coconut flour, baking soda, powdered xylitol, egg, coconut butter, and salt and blend throughly.

3. Form dough into ball. Place dough ball on a sheet of wax paper. Cover the ball with a second sheet of wax paper and flatten with a rolling pin to about 1/4" thick. Leave the dough on the wax sheet and place in refrigerator for about 1 hour.

4. Preheat oven to 325 degrees.

5. After dough has been refrigerated, set dough and wax sheets on the counter. Remove the top wax sheet. Using the top of a glass, a biscuit cutter, or cookie cutter, cut out cookies. Reshape dough into a flat sheet and continue cutting until all the dough is used. Gently place cookies on a cookie sheet.

6. Bake cookies for 15 minutes or until firm to the touch. The longer you bake them, the crunchier they will become. Let cool completely before removing from cookie sheet.

Directions for dessert crust:

1. Preheat oven to 375 degrees.

2. Measure xylitol first, and then grind it in a small electric coffee grinder or high powered blender (the coffee grinder makes a finer powder).

3. With a fork, combine almond flour, cacao powder, arrowroot powder, coconut flour, baking soda, powdered xylitol, egg, coconut butter, and salt and blend throughly.

4. Form dough into ball. Place dough ball in a pie tin or 9x9 pan. Flatten dough to form a crust.

5. Bake for 8-10 minutes or until firm to the touch. Let cool completely before adding ice cream filling.

Cookies and cream filling:

- 1/2 c. + 2 Tbs. coconut butter (a.k.a. coconut manna, coconut cream)
- 3 T. xylitol granules, powdered
- 2 Tbs. + 2 tsp. unsweetened nut milk (coconut, almond, cashew, etc.)
- 2 tsp. vanilla extract
- 1/4 tsp. stevia, to taste

Directions:

1. Measure xylitol first, and then grind it in a small electric coffee grinder or high powered blender (the coffee grinder makes a finer powder).

2. In a small bowl, combine coconut butter, powdered xylitol, nut milk, and vanilla extract. Blend throughly with a stick blender.

3. Add the stevia to the mixture - start with half of the stevia the recipe calls for, then add a little at a time until it's almost too sweet. (When the ice cream freezes, the sweetness factor subsides.)

4. Use for filling chocolate cookies or adding to ice cream.

COOKIES AND CREAM ICE CREAM

- 1 - 14 oz. unsweetened canned coconut milk
- 1 c. unsweetened nut milk (coconut, almond, cashew, etc.)
- 4 T. vanilla extract
- 1/4 c. xylitol granules, powdered
- a pinch of celtic sea salt
- 1/2 tsp. stevia, or to taste

Directions:

1. Measure xylitol first, and then grind it in a small electric coffee grinder or high powered blender (the coffee grinder makes a finer powder). Then combine canned coconut milk, nut milk, vanilla extract, xylitol powder, and salt and blend thoroughly.

2. Add the stevia to the mixture - start with half of the stevia the recipe calls for, then add a little at a time until it's almost too sweet. (When the ice cream freezes, the sweetness factor subsides.)

3. Pour mixture into the bowl of an ice cream machine. Add desired amount of crumbled chocolate cookies and cookie cream filling and freeze according to the manufacturer's instructions. After the ice cream is thickened, you can eat it

immediately or transfer it to an airtight container, cover tightly with a lid, and freeze until ready to serve.

4. Optionally, you can also pour the ice cream mixture directly into a freezer-safe bowl, cover with a lid, and freeze without the need for an ice cream machine (however, the ice cream will not be as creamy).

5. Let ice cream sit at room temperature for about 20 minutes before serving.

Or create these options:

1. Chocolate 'Oreo' Cookies: bake chocolate cookies, cool completely, then place a spoonful of cookies and cream filling between two cookies and press together gently.

2. Cookies N' Cream Dessert: bake chocolate crust, let cool completely, fill with cookies and cream ice cream, and freeze for 2 hours. Let ice cream sit at room temperature for about 20 minutes before serving.

3. Cookies N' Cream Ice Cream Sandwich: bake chocolate cookies, cool completely, then place a heaping spoonful of cookies and cream ice cream between two cookies and press together gently.

ICE TREATS

Avocado Pudding Pops

- 2 avocados, peeled and seed removed
- 1/2 c. raw cacao powder
- 3/4 c. nut milk (coconut, almond, cashew, etc.)
- 1 tsp. vanilla extract
- 1/2 tsp. almond extract
- 1/4 c. + 2 T. xylitol granules, powdered
- pinch of celtic sea salt
- 3/4 tsp. stevia, to taste

Directions:

1. Measure xylitol first, and then grind it in a small electric coffee grinder or high powered blender (the coffee grinder makes a finer powder).

2. In food processor, combine avocados, cacao powder, nut milk, vanilla extract, almond extract, xylitol powder, and salt and blend thoroughly.

3. Add the stevia to the mixture - start with half of the stevia the recipe calls for, then add a little at a time until it's almost too sweet. (When the pudding pops freeze, the sweetness factor subsides.)

4. Scoop pudding into popsicle molds and freeze for 2 hours or until solid.

Instant Strawberry Slush

- 1 - 14 oz. unsweetened canned coconut milk
- 1 c. unsweetened nut milk (coconut, almond, cashew, etc.)
- 4 c. frozen strawberries
- 2 T. vanilla extract
- 1 c. club soda
- 10 ice cubes
- 1/4 c. xylitol granules, powdered
- a pinch of celtic sea salt
- 1/2 tsp. stevia, or to taste

Directions:

1. Measure xylitol first, and then grind it in a small electric coffee grinder or high powered blender (the coffee grinder makes a finer powder).

2. In blender, combine canned coconut milk, nut milk, frozen strawberries, vanilla extract, club soda, ice cubes, xylitol powder, and salt. Blend thoroughly.

3. Add the stevia - start with half of the stevia the recipe calls for, then add a little at a time until it's to your taste.

Healthy Lemonade Popsicles

- 1 - 14 oz. unsweetened canned coconut milk
- 1 c. unsweetened nut milk (coconut, almond, cashew, etc.)
- 1 1/3 c. fresh squeezed lemon juice (about 6 lemons)
- 2 Tbs. raw apple cider vinegar (with 'the mother')
- 1/4 c. xylitol granules, powdered
- a pinch of celtic sea salt
- 1/2 tsp. stevia, or to taste

Directions:

1. Measure xylitol first, and then grind it in a small electric coffee grinder or high powered blender (the coffee grinder makes a finer powder).

2. In a blender, combine canned coconut milk, nut milk, lemon juice, apple cider vinegar, powdered xylitol, and salt and blend thoroughly.

3. Add the stevia to the mixture - start with half of the stevia the recipe calls for, then add a little at a time until it's almost too sweet. (When the popsicles freeze, the sweetness factor subsides.)

4. Pour mixture into the bowl of an ice cream machine. Freeze according to the manufacturer's instructions. After the ice cream is thickened. Pour into popsicle molds or ice cube trays and freeze for 2 hours or until solid.

5. Optionally, you can also pour the ice cream mixture directly into popsicle molds or ice cube trays, and freeze without the need for an ice cream machine (however, the popsicles will not be as creamy).

Pau D' Arco Popsicles

- 1/4 c. Pau D' Arco bark
- 16 oz. near boiling water
- 1 - 14 oz. unsweetened canned coconut milk
- 1 c. unsweetened nut milk (coconut, almond, cashew, etc.)
- 2 Tbs. vanilla extract
- 1/4 c. xylitol granules, powdered
- a pinch of celtic sea salt
- 1/2 tsp. stevia, or to taste

Directions:

1. Combine Pau D' Arco bark and hot water, set aside for 10 minutes to steep.

2. Measure xylitol first, and then grind it in a small electric coffee grinder or high powered blender (the coffee grinder makes a finer powder).

3. In a blender, combine Pau D' Arco tea, canned coconut milk, nut milk, vanilla extract, powdered xylitol, and salt and blend thoroughly.

4. Add the stevia to the mixture - start with half of the stevia the recipe calls for, then add a little at a time until it's almost too sweet. (When the popsicles freeze, the sweetness factor subsides.)

5. Pour mixture into the bowl of an ice cream machine. Freeze according to the manufacturer's instructions. After the ice cream is thickened. Pour into popsicle molds or ice cube trays and freeze for 2 hours or until solid.

Optionally, you can also pour the ice cream mixture directly into popsicle molds or ice cube trays, and freeze without the need for an ice cream machine (however, the popsicles will not be as creamy).

Eggnog Dessert

Gingersnap Dessert Crust:
(Recipe from The Sweeter Side of Candida)

- 1 1/2 c. almond flour, room temperature
- 8 Tbs. coconut oil, melted
- 1 1/2 tsp. ginger powder
- 1/2 tsp. cinnamon
- stevia to taste
- pinch of salt

Directions:

1. Preheat oven to 375 degrees.
2. In a small mixing bowl, combine ingredients with a fork or pastry cutter and press into a pie plate or 9x9 pan.
3. Bake for 8-10 minutes or until firm to the touch. Let cool completely before adding ice cream filling.

EGGNOG ICE CREAM:

- 1/2 c. chopped pecans, toasted
- 1 - 14 oz. unsweetened canned coconut milk
- 1 c. unsweetened nut milk (coconut, almond, cashew, etc.)
- 2 T. vanilla extract
- 1 tsp. rum extract
- 1 tsp. nutmeg
- 1/4 c. xylitol granules, powdered
- a pinch of celtic sea salt
- 1/2 tsp. stevia, or to taste

Directions:

1. Place pecans on cookie sheet and toast at 325 degrees for 15 minutes until just lightly browned. Set aside to cool.

2. Measure xylitol first, and then grind it in a small electric coffee grinder or high powered blender (the coffee grinder makes a finer powder). Then combine canned coconut milk, nut milk, vanilla extract, rum extract, nutmeg, xylitol powder, and salt and blend thoroughly.

3. Add the stevia to the mixture - start with half of the stevia the recipe calls for, then add a little at a time until it's almost too sweet. (When the ice cream freezes, the sweetness factor subsides.)

4. Pour mixture into the bowl of an ice cream machine. Freeze according to the manufacturer's instructions. After the ice cream is thickened, pour over dessert crust, then sprinkle with toasted pecans. Cover tightly with a lid and freeze about 2 hours or until ready to serve.

    Optionally, you can also pour the ice cream mixture directly into a freezer-safe bowl, sprinkle with toasted pecans, cover with a lid, and freeze without the need for an ice cream machine (however, the ice cream will not be as creamy). Once the ice cream is semi-frozen, scoop out and place over dessert crust. Cover tightly with a lid and freeze about 2 hours or until ready to serve.

5. Let ice cream sit at room temperature for about 20 minutes before serving.

Butterscotch -Vanilla Float

- 1/2 c. hot water
- 1/2 Tbs. gelatin
- 4 T. butter
- 10 ice cubes
- 1/2 c. club soda
- 1 tsp. vanilla extract
- stevia to taste
- vanilla ice cream

Directions:

1. In a blender, combine hot water, gelatin, and butter. While blending, drop in one ice cube at a time, taking about 1 minute to add all the ice cubes. Let the mixture blend for about 5 minutes until it becomes frothy and slightly thick.

2. Add club soda and vanilla extract and blend. Add stevia, to preferred sweetness.

3. Scoop vanilla ice cream into glasses and pour mixture overtop.

Candida-Dilly Bars

Chocolate Dip:

- 1 c. coconut oil
- 1/2 c. raw cacao powder
- 1/4 c. xylitol granules, powdered
- pinch of celtic sea salt
- stevia, to taste
- vanilla ice cream
- variety of toppings (unsweetened coconut flakes, sliced almonds, chopped pecans, etc.)

Directions:

1. Prepare a batch of vanilla ice cream. Scoop ice cream into popsicle molds and insert popsicle sticks. Freeze for at least 2 hours.

2. Measure xylitol first, and then grind it in a small electric coffee grinder or high powered blender (the coffee grinder makes a finer powder).

3. In a small saucepan, melt coconut oil, cacao powder, xylitol powder, salt, and stevia. Set aside to let cool.

4. While chocolate dip is cooling, gently remove popsicles from mold by running under lukewarm water and gently wiggling out. Place on a plate and return to freezer for at least 1 hour.

5. Pour chocolate dip into a tall container, like a coffee mug, tall enough to dip the popsicle into.

6. Remove popsicles from freezer and dip quickly into chocolate dip. Return to

freezer for about 10 minutes. Re-dip 2-3 more times to get a nice layer. On your last dip, sprinkle with desired toppings.

7. Store in freezer until ready to serve.

Does your struggle with candida seem to be taking over your life? You're making healthier food choices, yes, but it doesn't seem to completely shake the recurring infections, the brain fog, the moodiness, or remove the weight that's still hanging on.

Did you know that changing your food choices is only 50% of healing your gut and taking care of candida? Candida doesn't only thrive on the foods you eat, but on every aspect of your life style.

The hard part? Knowing what to change and finding someone to walk you through a plan of action

Until now.

At WholeIntentions.com, your health is priority. The Kicking Candida Program offers 7 full months of 1-on-1 coaching through an entire candida protocol created to heal you from top to bottom and inside out.

If you want to heal your gut and drop the weight, visit Kicking Candida.com to learn more!

"...very relevant lifestyle choices that we can make to enhance **the health and the diversity of the gut bacteria**. That's going to give us a lifelong advantage in terms of being resistant to the very diseases that we dread the most."

~ Dr. Perlmutter - neurologist

Made in the USA
Middletown, DE
30 January 2019